THE GREAT TRIBULATION SURVIVAL GUIDE FOR THOSE LEFT BEHIND

MICHAEL W. DEWAR, SR.

Copyright © 2021 by Michael W. Dewar, Sr.

All rights reserved. No Part of this book may be reproduced in any form without permission of the author or publisher.

Published in the United States by:
Dwelling Place Cleansing
PO Box 360196
Brooklyn, New York 11236

Dpscleansing.com

ISBN: 978-1-7334-3777-6

Scripture quotations are generally taken from the New International Version (NIV) Copyright © 1973, 1978, 1984, 2011 by International Bible Society. Used by permission. All rights reserved. Where other sources are used, the acronym of the translation is indicated (e.g., KJV, NKJV, ESV). Copyright Page.

CONTENTS

Preface..v

Introductions...9

1. The Gone and the Left Behind............................15
2. Life on Earth When the Church is Gone..............25
3. The Nature of the Great Tribulation...................31
4. Can I Survive without Taking the Mark of the Beast?...45
5. How to Refuse the Mark of the Beast and Survive........53
6. Will Raptured People Return to Earth?.....................71
7. Kingdom Age Begins...81

  Appendix A: Your Quality of Life In Hiding...............91

  Appendix B: When to Exit Your Hiding Place............97

  Other Books by this Author......................................101

PREFACE

Dear Brothers and Sisters,

You are reading this survival guide because multitudes of us Christian believers are missing globally. We have left earth for heaven in what is commonly known as "the rapture" (to be caught up), and multitudes of weeping humanity are the left behind. Or perhaps, the Church has not yet left the earth, we are still here.

Whether we are gone or still here, this guide was prepared for you. If we are still here, you need know what is coming that you can plan to leave with us when the rapture occurs. If we are already gone and you are among the *left behind*, you need to know what you must now do to survive short term and long term.

This guide is written from the perspective that the Church is already gone, and you are left behind. Life is going to be extremely difficulty upon the earth for seven years; you must urgently make a survival plan. This book is your guide, roadmap, and compass in formulating that plan. It puts you on the fast track and provides the information on the things you need to know and do quickly. This is not a book to quickly skim through and throw aside. It contains life-saving information; it is your survival guide. Don't lose it!

Believers all over the world are expecting a trumpet call from heaven for some time now (1Thess.4:16). Once this occurs, the *Great Exodus* commonly known as the *Rapture* will happen for those that are genuine believers in Jesus Christ. If you are not a believer and follower of Jesus Christ, you will not hear the trumpet call and you will not see or hear anything unusual until we are gone and reported missing. There will be worldwide pandemonium within nations and among broadcast media people everywhere.

You know we are still here because no news media has yet reported Christians missing locally or globally. Either way, this guide is a beneficial document to have in your possession; it contains a glut of important information you ought to know. Read it carefully to get yourself rapture-ready, and if you get *left behind*, follow it closely to know what to do in this time of trouble.

Let me be frank with you up front, your best survival chance is to be *Rapture* ready now! This way you can leave with us the moment that trumpet sounds. The call to leave is imminent; it can happen anytime, anywhere: at midnight or midday, at twilight or at dawn when sunlight through darkness. It can happen while you are going to work, at work or coming from work, while you are shopping or at church. That is what imminent means; it can happen anytime.

Speaking of readiness, the Lord Jesus said:

Therefore, keep watch, for in such an hour when you think not the Son of Man will come. If the owner of the house had known at what time of the night the thief was coming, he would have kept watch and would not let his house be broken into. So, you also must be ready, because the Son of Man will come at an hour when you do not expect him. (Matt.24:43-44 NIV)

Departure from earth will be so fast and so sudden, there will be no time for preparation. It will happen in the "twinkling of an eye"(1Cor.15:51-52). That is, perhaps, faster than or as fast as the speed of light (Matt.24:27). Postponing spiritual preparedness is nothing short of playing Russian Roulette with your eternal destiny. Now is the time to set your spiritual house in order before the time of trouble is upon you. You get ready by asking God to forgive the wrongs of your life, then invite Jesus into your life as Savior and Lord.

INTRODUCTION
The Day of Trouble

The second book of the Bible is called, Exodus, because it deals with the departure (going out) of the Children of Israel, the ancient people of God, from 400 years of Egyptian slavery under the leadership of Moses. He brought them to a safe place. That safe place was Canaan, the Land of Promise, the land of corn and wine, milk and honey. The Exodus was a real historical event, but it has at least two spiritual applications that concern us today.

First, it signifies the deliverance of the sinner from the bondage of sin through Jesus; that is our escape from spiritual Egypt and the walk of faith in Jesus Christ (Matt.11:28-30). Allegorically, this walk of faith is beautifully captured in John Bunyan's classic work, *The Pilgrim's Progress* in which the character, Christian, is depicted fleeing the *City of Destruction* to the *Celestial City*.

Second, the Exodus also typifies the literal, end-time departure of the people of God from earth to heaven when Jesus calls for them through the trumpet blast of an archangel (1Thes.4:16-18). This event is commonly referred to by Christians as *the rapture*, the catching away of the true Church.

This book does not debate the theological issues surrounding the *Rapture* and the Second Coming of Jesus to planet earth. Those issues are sufficiently dealt with in numerous scholarly works already on the market. The time for debates and speculations are long gone. The world is facing a time of unprecedented crisis and before you know it, every man is going to be for himself.

Survival is going to be the key concern of everyone. The time is now critical, the atmosphere is saturated with the spirit of urgency. What are *left-behind* people going to do? They need to survive, but surviving is not enough. They need to escape hell itself. They need to avoid taking the *Mark of the Beast* because that is a one-way ticket to hell. It looks like the last train has left earth, and you need a ticket for heaven; that is the primary issue this book is concerned with.

For that reason, this work is not written to the scholarly community for debate, but to ordinary people in crisis who want more than survival. Yes, they want to physically survive the crisis. But they also want a ticket to the *eternal life,* such as the raptured group that left for heaven has secured for themselves. I classify the left-behinders into two large groups of people: unbelievers and false

INTRODUCTION

believers. This book is written for these two groups. After describing each, however, I treat them as one group: the left-behinders.

First, the unbelievers. These are people of various classifications: atheists, agnostics, skeptics, and just plain ordinary unbelieving folks. You are the persons that don't usually go to church or pay too much attention to spiritual things, especially Christian spirituality. To date, you consider such things, nonsense, and the embracers of such lifestyle misguided and hypocritical people, and perhaps, many of them were. But most of them are gone and you are here. We know you are going to need all the help you can get, but you must act fast because things are going to move from bad to worse in a hurry. This book is for you; it is your survival guide.

Second, this book is written for false believers. You are what the preceding group calls, hypocrites. Some of you are preachers, deacons, tele-evangelist, miracle workers, divinity school professors, and regular church members. You all call yourselves Christian believers. But you were not living right and that is why you are left behind. You were not walking as directed by the holy scriptures and the blessed Holy Spirit and you are left behind with the rest of sinners. How foolish, how sad, that of all people you are here! Now what are you going to do?

All of you *left-behinders* listen up! I have bad news and I have good news. The bad news you are already experiencing, and it is going to get *badder*; I mean, much worst. The good news is, you still have a second chance to make it to heaven and even survive this time of trouble physically alive. *But it is not going to be easy!*

To make it to heaven, you must rectify your relationship with Jesus Christ and *refuse the Mark of the Beast* at all costs; choose death over the *Mark of the Beast.* If you refused the *Mark of the Beast* your chance of surviving without being killed is slim to none. If you want to retain that slim survival chance, be very shrewd during this time of trouble and give close attention to the guidance given in this book. It is written primarily for spiritual and physical survival purposes. In other words, your life now and hereafter are at risk.

Here are three quick suggestions for you: 1) don't panic, because that could put yourself in more danger; calm down and use your head from here onward. 2) Do not run to any church building for help; stay away from them. The people who could help you are gone. Satan has taken control of church buildings and all places of worship. 3) Get hold of a small Bible you can easily hide; Just *the New Testament* (NT) is fine. What you need to know is in the NT.

The electronic Bible on your phone will not do, and soon you will have to get rid of your phone. Your phone has a tracking device that the authorities will use to locate you when they are ready for you. The Bible and this book are your road map. The group of "unbelievers" spoken of earlier needs follow the three quick

INTRODUCTION

suggestions as well. You are all *Left-behinders*, you are now one group; all that is said in this book is for you.

So, how do you know you are left behind? It will be no secret! The worldwide print and broadcast news media will be preoccupied with it for weeks, trying to explain the conundrum of millions of people suddenly missing from earth. The news media will bring out their experts to explain what has happened, but there is only one book on earth that has the explanation and the people to explain it are gone. The Bible is a spiritual book, and the blessed Holy Spirit is needed to understand it. Unbelievers do not have the Holy Spirit so they cannot explain the Bible accurately. For that reason, we have prepared this book for you; it gives you all the explanation you need to know. Don't listen to any so-called expert. The experts are gone!

The one thing all the missing people have in common is the fact that they are all Christians; they have been followers of Jesus Christ from every nation, language, people, and race. People you know, perhaps, are among the missing.

Now, time is of the essence; you have none to waste. You must spring into action with a few of your closest friends and dependable family members to form a trusted survival team.

I want you to immediately understand what has happened, why you are left here, and what you must do to achieve the relationship with the Lord Jesus that the missing folks have, and what you must now do to stay alive without starving to death, killed, caught, and branded for hell with the *Mark of the Beast*. This is the everyday challenge that you must face from here onward.

There are those people who may want to take the martyrdom route out of this; that is, they are willing to die going out to win others to Jesus. That's noble, but don't make a fool of yourself. You are left behind because your relationship with the Lord was not right. Your primary goal now is to make it right by surrendering your life to Jesus. If you want to fight the system to bring others to Jesus, you will be killed in short order. Again, that's noble, but you don't know how you will respond if you are tortured before they kill you. If you break and take the *Mark of the Beast*, you throw away your life and heaven.

But if you want to give your life that way to the Lord, that's fine, but all the members on your team must commit themselves to the same. You can use this guide and adjust it for your purpose. I will make mention of a martyrdom team no more through the rest of this book. To be clear, this book is primarily written for people who want to make it to heaven through knowing Jesus as Savior and Lord and if possible, physically survive the Great Tribulation without taking the *Mark of the Beast*. These two things your only goals and purpose.

CHAPTER 1
The GONE AND THE LEFT BEHIND

Who are the people that are gone, and who are those that are left? Why are some people gone and others are left? This chapter seeks to understand these two fundamental questions and, in that context, guide you to achieve the same status of knowing Jesus as those that are gone and provide information to help you survive an evil system that will control the world for seven years.

While it is important to survive, survival is not the most import thing. Most people will survive by permanently pledging their allegiance to Satan. The most important thing is to achieve the coveted status of those that are gone. You achieve that status by clinging to Jesus Christ and resist taking the *Mark of the Beast* at all costs because by taking the *Mark of the Beast*, you give your allegiance to Satan, and it cannot be reversed.

By giving your allegiance to Jesus Christ instead of Satan, you are most likely to lose your physical life, the Beast will have you killed. But everyone that loses his or her life for Jesus Christ will find it again (Matt.10:39). You find your life again by not fearing those who can only destroy the body and can do no more but fear God who can "destroy both body and soul in hell" (v.28).

The Crowd that is Gone

The multitude that is gone from earth to heaven are the righteous, the people of God from the past to the present time. They fall into two main groups: the righteous dead (they died in the Lord) and the righteous living (1Thess. 4:16-18).

The term the righteous dead is not an accurate expression; the correct term is the righteous who have died. They are no more dead because they have been brought back to life. This group is consisted of all righteous people who have died from the time of Adam and Eve to the present time. They have all been resurrected and this resurrection is called, the first resurrection. You want to live now in such a way that if you die before the Lord comes, you can be in the first resurrection as those that are gone.

Jesus said He is the resurrection and the life. The person who believes in him will never dies, but if he dies, he will live again (John 11:25-26). Jesus speaks of two resurrections in these words, "Do not be amazed at this, for a time is coming when all who are in their graves will hear his voice and come out—those who have done what is good will rise to live, and those who have done what is evil will rise to be condemned" (John 5:28-29 NIV).

There are two resurrections spoken of in the preceding quote: the resurrection of the righteous and the resurrection of the wicked (i.e., unbelievers). These two resurrections are at least one thousand years apart. The resurrection of unbelievers is spoken of in Revelation 20:11-15. Our focus here is on the resurrection of the righteous dead (i.e., believers who have died in the Lord).

When Jesus calls for the Church at the time of the rapture, the living righteous will be caught up into heaven with the resurrected ones. Note again, the passage referenced earlier in 1Thessalonians 4:16-17 (NIV) says, "the dead in Christ shall arise first" (v.16). "After that, we who are still alive and are left will be caught up[raptured] together with them in the clouds to meet the Lord in the air…" (v.17). Two groups become one: the righteous dead resurrected, and the living righteous). This whole phenomenon is referred to as the "first resurrection" (Rev.20:5-6).

Both the resurrected group and the living group will be given heavenly bodies like the resurrection body of Jesus (1John 3:1-2). Jesus' resurrection body was real; it was not a phantom or ghost (John 20:26-28). The apostle Paul refers to this new body as "imperishable" and "immortal," it cannot get sick, diseased or die any more (1 Cor.15:51-58). He also refers to the believers' new body as a "building [from] God, an eternal house from heaven, not build by human hands," "our heavenly dwelling" (2 Cor.5:1-4). This new body is not a dirt house like our previous body, and it is not subject to the limitations of our dirt body.

So, the multitude of people that are missing are the righteous ones who believe in Jesus Christ, accepted His gift of salvation, and made Him Savior and Lord of their lives. They are not alone; the righteous of all ages who died are resurrected to join them in this great Exodus from earth to heaven.

Before we discuss the *left behind group* proper, let's answer the question, why God decides to move His people from earth to heaven? Are they running from something?

Why Are They Gone?

They are gone because they are true believers with a covenant relationship with God. God has obligated Himself to them. You are left behind because you are an *unbeliever* and falls outside the covenant of grace. But it is your choice that gives you that status.

Understand this—the God of the Bible is by nature a relational Being. Essential to His moral character are the attributes of love, justice, and mercy. His relationship with humankind is always based upon these three attributes in the context of covenant. For this reason, among others, He is the covenant-making and covenant-keeping God. Notice that the Bible is divided into Old Testament and New Testament. The word "testament" means "Covenant" or "Will."

The terms of a covenant are most often permanent and binding. At its core, a covenant is a conditional or unconditional promise to which both parties obligate themselves. A conditional promise is always prefaced with the word, "if" (stated or implied). If you do this, I will do that. For example, "If my people who are called by my name will humble themselves, and pray, and seek my face, and turn from their wicked way, I will hear from heaven, forgive their sins and heal their land (2Chron.7:14). The conditions of this promise are clear and simple. You do these things, and I will do these.

Now, here is a close unconditional promise in which God called Abraham away from his community and people to a new land and said to him:

> I will make you into a great nation, and I will bless you; I will make your name great, and you will be a blessing. I will bless those who bless you, and

whoever curse you I will curse; and all peoples on the earth will be blessed through you. (Gen.12:2-3).

A clear series of conditional promises are set forth in Deuteronomy 28. Here God spells out his obligation to the Israelite through Moses and the Israelite's obligation to him, and what would happy if they fail to meet their obligation under the covenant. God has no problem keeping His word; He is good for it. He is a covenant-maker and a promise-keeper. Humans are the very opposite; we are not good promise-keepers, we break covenants, hence the high divorce rate.

God made a covenant with all who accepted His salvation rescue plan by coming into relationship Jesus Christ (John 3:16). It is a simple conditional promise; you repent of your sin, come to the place of rescue, and stay there. You come to Jesus and abide in Him (John 3:1-21, 15: 1-10). You meet the simple terms of the covenant and drawdown on its promised blessings. God has obligated Himself to get you out of harm's way to a place of safety. This is the fundamental reason true believers are raptured to heaven and *unbelievers* and *false believers* are left behind. God is simply being faithful to His covenant and keeping His promise.

God is compelled by His own righteousness to make good on the promise. When humans doubt the promise of their fellow humans, they backup their promise with an oath or collateral. To make us comfortable God did the same (Heb.6:13-18). God has decided not to pour out His wrath upon His own people or chastise them with the wicked. That is true under both testaments.

When God decided to execute judgment upon the world of Noah's generation, He warned them a long time, but they ignored the warning. God made provision of protection for righteous Noah and his family. It was God himself who closed the door of the Ark (Gen.7:15-16; Matt.24:37-39). Lot and his family were pulled out of Sodom before God rain fire and brimstone on the twin city. God made it clear that He would not judge the righteous with wicked. God has not appointed his children unto wrath (Gen.18:16-33). There is no judgment to them who are in Christ Jesus (Rom.8:1).

The Great Tribulation is a time when the wrath of God will be poured out upon unbelieving humans and the earth that supports life. This will be a series of measured, apocalyptic judgments, as seen in the book of Revelation. They are poured out upon wicked humans to drive them to repentance before the final *Day of Judgment*. These judgments will be administered by Jesus Himself as He breaks a seven-seal scroll handed to Him in heaven (Rev.6-7).

Believers will not be here on earth to experience these judgments because Jesus has already suffered in their place on the cross (Isaiah 53:4-6). As a result, there is no Judgment or wrath to those who are in Christ Jesus (Romans 8:1-2). That is one major reason the bridegroom will call for His Bride before judgment is poured out upon the earth of unbelievers to move them to repentance and bring them into covenant relationship with Jesus.

The Multitudes Left Behind

Most of humanity will be left behind, billions of people; among them will be millions of so-called good people, good by this world's standard. By God's standard, there are no good people outside of Jesus Christ. There is none righteous, no not one. All have sinned and come short of the glory of God (Rom.3:9-18).

God in His mercy has made provision for all humankind to be saved. That is what John 3:16 is all about, "For God so love the world that he gave his one and only Son that whoever believes in Him should not perish but have eternal life." But the vast multitude of humankind rejects God's provision and choose their own way. Broad is the way that leads to destruction, and many find it. But narrow is the way that leads to life, and few find it (Matt.7:13-14). People choose their own way and most often, it is not God's way (Isaiah 53:6, 55:8-9). That is why they are left behind to face judgment with the hope that they will repent and be saved and not have to face God at the final white throne judgment (Rev.20:11-15).

In the introduction, I divided the left behind into two large groups: the *unbelievers* and some believers who were not living by God's standard. These so-called believers did not fully commit their lives to Jesus, that's why they are left behind. Some occasionally went to church but had one foot in the world and another in the church. They lived by the world's standard. Some of them know the Bible very well. There will be a lot of preachers among them, men and women who were in the ministry for fame, money, and power, not out of love for the Lord and people. Some will already know what to do to survive, but it will be very difficult to know who to trust.

Among the unbelievers are diehard Satan followers; they want nothing to do with God and Jesus Christ. They have given their allegiance to Satan, and they will work for Satan to compel all admirers of Christ to follow Satan. These hard-core Satanist will be in full charge of government, commerce, monetary exchange, law enforcement and administration justice. They will be in charge of institutions like the local police, FBI, CIA, Secret Service, and the private sector. Frankly, there will hardly be a private sector; all of life will be government managed, even institutions of worship.

Government will attach a biometric mark on all humans. It will be a barcode like number on your right hand or on your forehead, commonly called *the Mark of the Beast* (Rev.13:16-18). Without this mark or number, you cannot work to earn your keep, you cannot bank, do business, travel, buy or sell. If you are caught trying to get by without it, you will be arrested and have it forced on you. If you still refuse, you will be executed.

It will be most difficult for people with dependent children because your movement will be greatly restricted, and you cannot easily hide without being discovered. To abandon you children to save yourself is hardly an option, but some parents will be forced to do that. Food will be used as a means of control; to buy food, your government ID is required (i.e., *Mark of the Beast*). Hunger is a painful way to die; most parents don't have the heart to watch their children starve to death, knowing food is available. You can see how parents will take the mark so their children can eat. But it is not a long-term solution because the *Beast's Mark* cancels out eternal life.

Family will betray family; friends will betray friends. You will hardly know who to trust because government secret service police will be everywhere as well as paid informants. People who are in hiding must have massive amount of food supply and water to stay in their hiding place for years or be where you can live off the land.

Once you emerge from your hiding place, you compromise it for everyone because you are likely to be caught, forced to comply with the authorities or be killed. From your hiding place or anywhere close to it, you should not use any communication technology, such as cell phones or computers for they are equally compromising, unless you have expert encryption, cyber skills to prevent the authorities tracking your where abouts.

CHAPTER 2

LIFE On EARTH WHEN THE CHURCH IS GONE

To grasp the magnitude and intensity of conditions upon the earth when the Church is gone, a person must first grasp the true significance of the current presence of the Church in the world, the nature of the *Great Tribulation*, what Satan really wants, and the purpose of God. We will briefly cover these four things in this chapter at warp speed, so you can get a clear view of what life will be like.

The Presence of the Church

The presence and role of the Church in the world is largely taken for granted; most of us never lived in a society without the influence of the Church. But one day, the Church will be gone, and upon her sudden departure, all hell with break loose. Church buildings will still be standing on the corners as usual, and people will be entering them to worship, but most of the familiar faces that used to gather in them will be gone. The new worshippers are Satan's people; he controls the church buildings now, and the pastors are converting people to Satan.

When I speak of the Church, I am referring to the collective *People of God* from all Christian faith traditions who have come to salvation in Jesus Christ. Jesus refers to them as being "born again" (John 3:3-7). These people are registered in the Lamb's book of life in heaven (Heb.12:22-24; Rev.20:15). The apostle Peter refers to them as "a chosen people, a royal priesthood," "a holy nation, "a people belonging to God" (1Peter 3:9). They represent the kingdom of God on earth. Few of them are to be found in just every Christian church or denomination; their full number is known only to God.

Jesus informs us that this community of people serves as light and salt to the world (Matt.5:13-16). What does He mean? Without natural light we could see nothing in the physical world; it would be utter darkness. For that reason, light is the first creative act of God (Gen.1:3-5). God Himself is "light" and is also referred to as a "consuming fire" (1John 1:4-9; Heb.12:29). Light also speaks of godly reasoning, righteous knowledge; these qualities come to humans through Jesus Christ; He is the light that lightens every human that comes into the world (John 1:1-9). This light of reason, this righteous, godly knowledge is what gives humans ascendency over the brute creation. This is referred to as the image of God (Gen.1:26-27).

The Church is God's spiritual light to the masses of humanity, just as the heavenly lights illuminate the natural world. Anywhere the true knowledge of God is present, people thrive because they have the light of God. Jesus is the personified light of God. To reject Jesus and His gospel is to reject the righteous light of God and remain in spiritual darkness and ignorance (John 3:16-21).

The Church, the Christian community, the people of God serve not only as light to the masses of humanity (the world) but as salt of the world. Salt has a different function to light. Salt is a preservative that prevents decay; it gives flavor to things, and it creates thirst. The Holy Spirit resides in the Church since His grand entrance on the Day of Pentecost AD 33 in First century Jerusalem (Acts 1:8, 2: 1-7). His presence gives the Church the three efficacious powers of salt stated in this paragraph.

Salt is a preservative that prevents decay. The presence of the people of God in the world, prevents the worse in deprave humanity from being manifested. Noah's world, Sodom and Gomorrah, Babylon and Rome are biblical examples of the moral decay that can take place in a society without God or a society that tries to destroy the people of God. The apostle Paul tells us of the lawlessness that will break in like a compromised flood gate when the Church and the Holy

Spirit are gone from the earth. The lawless one (antichrist), the son of perdition will step out of the shadows to take control (2Thess.2:1-12).

Salt gives flavor to things. In other words, the people of God give flavor to the world; they make life more pleasant and desirable. They are by nature law abiding, forgiving, compassionate and charitable. Why? Because they live by the divine mandate to love God and neighbor (Matt.5:43-48). The new commandment that Jesus established is the law of love. Biblical love (agape) has great restraining powers and more so when exercised under the guidance of the indwelling Holy Spirit.

When the Church is gone, you are left with a world where people have no restraint against wickedness and cruelty. Just before God destroyed the people of Noah's day, it was said, "violence fills the earth, and every imagination of man's heart was evil continually" (Gen.6:5-8). According to Jesus, this condition will repeat itself in the time of the end, just before the return of the Lord (Matt.24:37-39). I suspect the conditions will be a thousand times worse than the days of Noah, because we have sophisticated technology and weapons of mass destruction to behave more wickedly. We now have the capability to remotely kill millions of people without impunity.

Finally, Salt creates thirst. For that reason, you desire water to quench your thirst. But now the salt is gone and there is no more appetite or thirst for the things of God. The animal nature is now unrestrained to gratify itself, and moral decay dominates. The unbridled passion of Sodom and Gomorrah will pale into insignificance as the nature of the brute beast governs the behavior of humankind. The Church as light is gone; the Church as salt is gone; only darkness and moral decay remain.

Lawlessness Reigns

The head of government when the Church is gone is called the "lawless one" (2Thess.2:3-4). This is a very strange term to explain because the lawless one in these verses refers to Satan. But Satan is represented by the Beast, the antichrist personality, who represents the one-world system of government (Rev.13).

Widespread economic disparity and violence in society will be the chief factors precipitating the antichrist's takeover as a solution to global crises. The antichrist will impose strict control. Life will feel as if the whole world is under martial law. He will be brutal to nations, cities, communities, and individuals who oppose him.

Before the lawless one takes the reigns of global government, the traditional institutions of law will have broken down so badly, it will make 9/11 and the Capital insurrection look like they happened on the same day and like a Sunday picnic. It is because of this unbridled violence and leadership vacuum, people will be crying out, "send us a leader, we will accept him be he God or Satan!" The world has called for Satan, and he comes smiling, having a solution for everything. He becomes the law-and-order leader with absolute power to execute anyone on the spot who opposes him.

The irony is, the lawless one becomes the law. As the God of the universe became incarnate (put on flesh) to become Man in the person of Jesus Christ, Satan imitates becoming flesh in the person of the antichrist. In one sense, the antichrist is Satan incarnate. Why?

Satan knows that to work among humans for good or evil, you need a human body to work through. God did it and got humans to worship Him; Satan calculates that he can win human's loyalty by become one of them as well as God did in Jesus Christ. But he will not give them a choice; he will force the disloyal into compliance. Satan finds the right man, gives him his power, his throne, and his authority (Rev.13:1-4). In the United States we say, *one nation under God*. But now it is one world under Satan.

CHAPTER 3
THE NATURE OF THE GREAT TRIBULATION

The happenings described in this chapter will take place during a period referred to in scripture as the *"Great Tribulation"* or *"the time of Jacob's Trouble"* (Matt.24:21; Jer.30:7). It will be a period of seven years of intense suffering on earth, such as mankind has never seen since the history of humans on the earth or ever again will be.

The suffering will be greatly intensified in the second half of the 7 years. For that reason, some scholars limit the *Great Tribulation* to that latter 3 ½ years and designate its onset as the point the Church will be raptured. This is often referred to as "Mid-tribulation Rapture" (in short *Mid-trib. Rapture*). Those who say the Church will be raptured at the very beginning of the seven years are said to believe in "Pre-tribulation Rapture" (Pre-trib. Rapture). There is a third group that says the Church will go through the Great Tribulation and Raptured at the end to meet the Lord in the air, makes a quick turn-around back to earth. This group believes in the Post-tribulation Rapture. The most popular view is the Pre-tribulation Rapture, the view of this author, that the Church will be gone from the earth.

The Great Tribulation will be a time of widespread war, famine, disease, and death, as depicted by the *four-horsemen* of the apocalypse and the 7-seal judgments of Revelation chapters 6 to 9.

There will be great upheaval in nature from the heavenly bodies that will affect life on earth. The sun will scorch humankind, meteorites falling to the earth; there will be volcanic eruptions, massive earthquakes moving islands out of their places, and gigantic tsunamis (Rev.6:12-14). Life will be absolutely terrifying that people will call upon death to take them out of their misery (vv.15-17).

Much of vegetation will be destroyed, causing worldwide famine; much of marine life will also die, greatly limiting the sea as food source (Rev.8:7-9). Drinking water will be scarce (vv.10-11). The government will control whatever food is left and ration it out to people with the *Mark of the Beast*. You cannot work, buy, or sell anything without this government issued, biometric identification. It will be difficult to live off the land because most of it will be under God's judgment.

The Nature of Government

The world has been gradually moving to a *One-world government* and currency for a long time. But most people are oblivious to it, they have not taken notice. People are so busy trying to make a living and cope with societal difficulties that they hardly have the energy to pay attention to anything else. But like a puzzle, the pieces are available, just waiting to be put together. The three most powerful forces pushing nations in that direction are the need for capable leadership, security, and economic survival. These forces are interconnected.

The European Union (EU) is one example of nations moving to a *One world government*. At the writing of this book there were 27 nations in the EU; it would have been 28 but Britain chose to withdraw. The EU is a political-economic union. Nations give up some of their sovereignty to be part of the EU, the One-world government will have absolute sovereignty. The Church that normally oppose godless dictatorship is gone. Nations now surrender individual sovereignty for collective sovereignty. They are forced to surrender their sovereignty for strong leadership, security, and economic survival. The United States is already showing cracks in its democratic foundations; it can hardly govern itself. It is imploding.

This One world government in depicted in Daniel 7 but more extensively in Revelation 13 as a *seven head, ten-horn beast* with a blasphemous name written on each head (v.1). Why blasphemous names? It is a government that is anti-God. The beast is like a leopard (cunning), and its feet like a bear (clumsy in movement), and mouth like a lion (v.2). A lion's mouth means, it is irresistible, vicious, and devouring. The dragon (Satan) gives the beast his power, throne, and great authority. This means the One world government is vested with the full powers and authority of Satan. In other words, the President of this government will be Satan in the flesh as Jesus was God in the flesh. He is the strongman the world was waiting for.

This global, satanic leader will demonstrate that if you kill him, like Jesus, he will come back to life to deal with you. Note, that one of his seven heads suffered a fatal wound (v.3) but the wound was healed. This speaks of an assignation attempt that he survives. He is charismatic, charming, and mesmerizing; he marvels the whole world, and they gladly follow him. He will control the collective arm forces of the nations that surrender their sovereignty, and he will control the global economy.

When antichrist first appears on the global scene, he comes as the man of peace with the capability to solve the global crisis facing the nations. With his charm and eloquence, he deceives the whole world until his power is consolidated, then his true satanic character becomes apparent to all. But most people will not care that this is an evil man (Satan), they are charmed by his leadership. Those that refused to submit to his authority will suffer his wrath.

The Nature of Religion and Worship

During the *Great Tribulation,* government, politic, monetary system, religion, commerce, global economics, and the military industrial complex will be one satanic system of worship. To understand this, you must know what Satan wants. He wants three interrelated things.

First, Satan's aspiration is to be God with the big "G." He was a top executive in the government of God (an archangel). Scholars believe his ministry portfolio was worship; this includes music. Worship is everywhere in God's kingdom, especially in heaven. Worship is the food of God, so Lucifer was the head chef.

It was from this position that Lucifer led a coup d'état to overthrow God and was defeated. He lost his place in heaven and was expelled (Rev.12:7-12). But Satan has not abandoned his ambitious aspiration. He thinks he can still achieve his goal by defeating the second person of the blessed Holy Trinity, Jesus Christ. He is on a mission to defeats Jesus because he thinks that will qualify him for the throne. Satan is already spoken of in the Bible as the god of this world, but that is "god" with a small "g," and he is not satisfied with that. His sight is set higher than that and he is in it for the long haul.

Secondly, Satan wants the same thing God wants, "worship!" But Satan has no worship standard. How do I know this? Satan blew his cover in the temptation of Jesus, he sought to bribe Jesus to worship him. Matthew (4:8-10) gives us this intelligence report:

Again, the devil took him to a very high mountain, and showed him all the kingdoms of this world and their glory. And he said to him, 'All these I will give you, if you will fall down and worship me.' Then Jesus said to him, 'Be gone, Satan! For it is written, 'You shall worship the Lord your God and him only shall you serve.' (Matt.4:8-10 ESV)

God sets the standard of worship that He accepts in heaven and on earth (Isa.6:1-7; Rev.4-5). God through Moses, in the books of Exodus and Leviticus, sets the Standard of worship He accepts among the ancient Israelites. Aaron's two sons lost their lives when they deviated from that standard (Lev.10:1-11).

Jesus redefines God's acceptable standard of worship for New Covenant believers in the Sermon on the Mount (Matt.5-7). He said to His disciples, "...unless your righteousness exceeds that of the Scribes and Pharisees, you will never enter the kingdom of heaven" (Matt.5:20). Jesus called the Scribes and Pharisees hypocrites, for they set aside the Word of God and teach their own man-made tradition. He never had much to do with them. And they knew it and plotted to kill Him at the opportune time.

So, Satan wants to be worshipped and he has no established worship standard. He will pay you off to get it. He gets into churches and corrupt their worship, so it comes to him by default, because it falls short of God's standard. And most often church folks kept on worshipping, not knowing that their worship is not accepted by God. Like Israel retuning the Ark to Jerusalem on a new cart, thinking God was pleased with their worship until Uzzah fell dead (2 Sam.6:1-8).

For New Testament (NT) believers, Jesus is the standard of worship that God accepts. In fact, worship must be first approved by the blessed Holy Spirit, then handed off to Jesus our heavenly High Priest who directs it to the Father (John 4:21-24; Heb.8:1-2).

Third, Satan wants a kingdom with legitimacy; one that is recognized by heaven and earth. He appointed himself god of this world and has established his own kingdom; the Bible refers to it as the kingdom of darkness (Col.1:12-14). Satan is worse than the Taliban; he has an illegitimate government that is not recognized.

Angels and humans are forbidden to worship Satan. He cannot take over a human being without that person's permission. Any Holy Spirit anointed person can evict him. The devils that were evicted from the Gadara demoniac by Jesus, had to ask permission to get into pigs (Mark 5:1-14). That's how low the once mighty archangel Lucifer has fallen (Ezek.28:14-17; Isa. 14:12-15).

But at the time of the *Great Tribulation*, when the Holy Spirit raptures the Church from earth to heaven, Satan for the first time will think, finally, I have gotten some respect. He is allowed full control of this world to establish his own government and compel worship. Only God has full control, but Satan will think that he has full control.

Revelation 13:8 states, "All the inhabitants of the earth will worship the beast—all whose names have not been written in the Lamb's book of life, the Lamb who was slain from the creation of the world" (NIV). But wait this is just the beginning of Satan's political, economic, governmental worship system.

The Nature of Law Enforcement (Rev.13:11-18)

The second beast that we are going to look at in this section is fundamentally about deadly law enforcement. The apostle John gives us the following intelligence report of what's happening on earth at about the mid-point (3 ½ years in) of the Great Tribulation:

> Then I saw a second beast, coming out of the earth. It had two horns like a lamb, but it speaks like a dragon. It exercised all the authority of the first beast on its behalf, and the earth and its inhabitants to worship the first beast, whose fatal wound had been healed. And it performed great signs, even causing fire to come down from heaven to earth in full view of people. Because of the signs…it deceived the inhabitants of the earth…It also force all people, great and small, rich and poor, free and slaves, to receive a mark on their right hands or on their forehead, so that they could not buy or sell unless they had the mark, which is the name of the beast or the number of his name. (Rev.13:11-17 NIV)

Now, let us analyze the character of this beast and his function. First, his deceptive character. He has two *horns like a lamb*. This means, in appearance he looks harmless. *But he speaks like a dragon* (Satan). He is not to be trifled with; he has all the authority of Satan. This person is a respected religious, political authority like an archbishop, cardinal, or an evil Pope. Bible scholars gives him the title, *The False Prophet*. He comes out of the apostate church.

The apostate church is depicted in Revelation 17 as a luxuriously decorated prostitute with a communion chalice in her hand, riding the seven head, ten horn, scarlet color beast. This is the same beast that opens Revelation 13. But this time the beast has the liturgical color of scarlet. In other words, she is in bed with Satan.

She is called a prostitute, because she has two lovers: Jesus and money, the unrighteous mammon. She is also referred to as the mother of harlots, meaning, she represents a lead denomination with many churches under her control doing the same thing (for more on her, see my book, *The Book of Life & The Books of Wrath*).

The job of the second beast (of Rev.13) is to enforce the policies of the first beast (of Rev.13) who is Satan in the flesh. Think of the first beast as the President and the second as the Attorney General who enforces the policies of the President, only this time the President is the leader of the One world Government. And his sidekick, the Attorney General, is to enforce his global policies.

Second, this beast controls and enforces the economic policy of the One world government, for no one can buy or sell without his permission. He issues a biometric government ID; it is bar coded on your right hand or on your forehead where it can be easily read by sight and or a bar code scanner.

Third, everything has to do with worship because that is what Satan desires most. The second beast is in charge of worship policy worldwide at the point of a gun. Life is about worshipping Satan whether you are rich or poor, great, or small, free or slave; you are force to be loyal to Satan. An image of the first beast will be made and installed in places of worship all over the world and people are forced to worship. The image will know each worshipper and it will be able to talk, walk, and shake hands at church. But it is not a real person; it is humanoid, artificial intelligence (AI). IBM has a computer named Watson that they have been perfecting for some time to compete with humans. So, don't think that this is far-fetched; this technology is already available.

Fourth, church people love miracles, they love to be mesmerized. Well, the second beast will satisfy this need for the miraculous. He will dazzle people with his tricks, even call down fire from heaven like the Prophet Elijah. Satan will sit as god in the house of God, showing himself to be god. People rejected the true God and His Christ too long, and for "this cause God shall send them strong delusion that they should believe a lie; that they all might be damned who believe not the truth but had pleasure in unrighteousness" (2 Thess. 2: 9-11 KJV). The apostate church is Satan's church, he will try to make it look as close to the true church as possible.

The Purpose of God

What is God's purpose during the *Great Tribulation*? First, God is not going to totally abandon the earth to Satan and unbelieving humans. God has a purpose in allowing Satan to have his way for a limited time. The fact is—Satan is not all-powerful, not all-knowing, or present everywhere as God. He may thing he is in full control of the earth, and he has Jesus against the ropes. But he is a finite being who is mistaken as he was with the man Job.

Satan was confident that Job would curse God, if Job is deprived of his wealth, his family, and his health (Job 1:9-12). God gave Satan permission to remove those things from Job's life and he did. But Job did not curse God, he praised God instead, proving Satan wrong (vv.20-22). Satan is not omniscient or omnipotent.

So, what is God's purpose for the *Great Tribulation*? For a long time, unbelieving humans wanted to be their own boss or to have a god on their terms. They wanted to make God in their own image and likeness. They have been trying this gone astray independence since the garden of Eden, trying to push God out of His world. Instead of God abandoning them, He provides redemption through His Son, Jesus Christ. But most humans refused God's grace.

They are hell-bent on serving Satan. So, God let them go ahead and serve Satan but not with all the refinements of heaven and earth that they have been accustomed. He withholds some of those goodies as judgment against them. It is as if God is saying, now let's see how well Satan will provide for you, how generous he can be to you, when the land and sea cut back on food supply.

The purpose of the *Great Tribulation* is to move sinful humankind to repentance and salvation in Jesus Christ. During this time, God will also turn his attention to Israel to prepare them to receive Jesus as their true Messiah as some have already done (Messianic Jews). As unbelieving as national Israel has been, God has not cast them away; eventually all Israel will be saved as the apostle Paul informs us in his discourse to the Romans (9-11).

Will the Great Tribulation accomplish God's purpose? The short answer is yes, millions of gentiles and Jews will repent and come to Jesus for Salvation. But most of them will pay with their lives at the hand of the Antichrist and the False prophet, whom Jesus will throw in hell upon His return to earth with the Church at the end of the *Great Tribulation* (Matt.24:29-31; Rev.19:11-16).

Satan will be arrested and put into prison for a thousand years (Rev.20:1-3). At the end of his prison term, Satan will be paroled for a short period, and he will use that time to reassemble his human followers to make one final assault on Jesus and His Church; fire comes down from heaven and devour all his human followers. Satan is finally thrown into hell where the Antichrist and the False prophet were thrown earlier (Rev.20: 7-10). Fallen human nature is rebellion against God, even when Satan is not around.

After this, the wicked dead will be resurrected to face judgment, as well as all living humans who continue to reject Jesus. Each human being dead or alive has a court date. The apostle John gives us the following intelligence report of the Final Judgment:

> Then I saw a great white throne and him who was seated on it. The earth and the heavens fled from his presence, and there was no place for them. And I saw the dead, great and small, standing before the throne, and the books were opened. Another book was opened, which is the book of life. The dead were judged according to what they had done as recorded in the books. The sea gave up the dead that were in it, and death and Hades gave up the dead that were in them, and each person was judged according to what they had done. Then death and Hades were thrown into the lake of fire. The lake of fire is the second death. Anyone whose name was not found written in the book of life was thrown into the lake of fire. (Rev.20:11-15 NIV)

So, all people dead or alive who reject the salvation God provides in His Son and serve Satan will be judged and thrown into hell to join Satan and his two sidekicks. Good riddance to Satan!

We kind of got a little ahead of ourselves, but to get you see the sequential unfolding of events it was necessary. Let's go back now to consider the question of surviving the *Great Tribulation* without taking the *Mark of the Beast*. Can it be done?

CHAPTER 4

CAN I SURVIVE WITHOUT TAKING THE MARK OF THE BEAST?

This is the million-dollar question many are asking; can I survive the seven years of *Great Tribulation* with the Antichrist and the False Prophet in charge of government without taking the mark of the beast? We will explore this question in this chapter, but I must tell you up front, this is not the most important question. The most important question is this: will I have the courage to refuse the *Mark of the Beast*? We will answer the second question first.

The Mark of the Beast

What is the mark of the beast and its purpose? We have partly answered this question already, but we are going to come at it from a different angle this time. We stated in Chapter 2 that *Mark of the Beast* is a biometric, government identification tattooed or barcoded to your right hand or your forehead. When scanned, it reveals just about everything about you. Our Social Security number serves a similar function, but not as comprehensive as the *Mark of the Beast*. The *Mark of the Beast* has four broad functions.

First, it serves as a government ID for controlling people. This we have sufficiently explained. Second, it has an economic function. You need it to work, to travel, to do business, to buy or sell. Since, the society is most likely cashless, your ID is digitally connected to your back account as your ATM card is now connected. You will not be able to get a quart of milk at the corner store without your ID or do anything else. The *Great Tribulation* will be a time of global food shortage; the government will control and ration what is available. Your ID, therefore, will be necessary just to get basic food supply. If you are a parent with small children, you must have food on a regular basis for them; that alone will force them to take the ID.

Third, the *Mark of the Beast* serves a spiritual function. It serves to mark those who belong to Satan. It is the outward sign of a person's allegiance to Satan; it indicates that you are permanently Satan's possession or property, even though the mark was forced on many. The Bible is clear that beast ID bearers and worshippers' names are not in the Lamb's book of life (Rev.13:8, 20:4).

CAN I SURVIVE WITHOUT TAKING THE MARK OF THE BEAST?

Allegiance to Jesus Christ is the only reason a person would refuse the *Mark of the Beast*. Having the mark will make life so much easier, in the short-term, because it is your pass or ID to travel, buy and sell, get food, and to access all government services.

But for the long-term (eternity) you have made yourself a child of Satan and a candidate for hell. So, refusing the Mark of the Beast, only make sense for those who have made a confession of faith in Jesus Christ. There comes the question, will a person be brave enough in the face of death to say, no, to taking the *Beast Mark?* Such refusal will take tremendous courage!

Refusing the mark is seen as defiance of the authority of government, and defiance of Satan's lordship and governance over your life on the one hand, and allegiance to Jesus Christ on the other hand. Such insubordination is punishable by death (Rev.13:15-17).

Death will not be easy; torture will precede it to convince people to change their minds. In view of this context, Jesus said don't be afraid of those who can only kill the body but can do no more. Fear God who can destroy the body and then throw you into hell (Matt.10:28). Again, He said, If you lose your life for His sake you will find it again (v.39).

Now, where Satan got this idea of placing ID marks of ownership on people? He learned it from God. Satan is not a creator; he is an imitator. He has no original ideas. His kingdom is patterned off the kingdom of his former employer whom he aspires to be, but never can be because he is a finite creature.

Circumcision in the Old Testament (OT) was, perhaps, God's first *mark of ownership* by covenant (Gen.17:9-16). Under the New Covenant, the Holy Spirit is given to those in Christ as a mark that we belong to God (Rom.8:9). The apostle Paul says it this way, "...When you believed [in Jesus], you were marked in him with a seal, the promised Holy Spirit of" (Eph.1:13).

During the Great Tribulation, God will seal in their foreheads 144,000 Jewish evangelists to preach the gospel, giving national Israel their last chance to receive Jesus as their Messiah (Rev.7:1-17,14:1-7). The apostle Paul said, "God's solid foundation stands firm, sealed with this inscription: 'The Lord knows those who are his'" (2Tim.2:19). There are other passages that indicate God sealing his own.

Satan copies this method, but for evil purposes. He forces his mark upon people and use it to control them. God respects the free will of people, and He gives a choice. But choices come with rewards and consequences. God tells the consequences up front (John 3:16).

Courage to Refuse the Mark of the Beast

The question is, will people have courage enough to embrace Jesus as their Savior and Lord and refuse the *Mark of the Beast*? The short answer is yes, many will surrender their lives to Jesus and receive the eternal salvation He provides. But sadly, untold millions will give their allegiance to Satan and be eternally lost; they will share Satan's eternal place in the lake of burning sulfur (Rev.20:10,13-15).

Now, how do we know that millions of gentiles and Jews will embrace Jesus as Savior and Lord and reject the Mark of the Beast unto death? The Word of God gives us this post-tribulation report:

> After this I looked, and therefore before me was a great multitude that no one could count, from every nation, tribe, people, and language, standing before the throne and before the Lamb. They were wearing white robes and were holding palm branches in their hands. And they cried out in a loud voice: 'Salvation belongs to our God, who sits on the throne, and to the Lamb....' Then one of the elders asked me, 'These in white robes—who are they; and where did they come from? I answered, 'Sir, you know...These are they who have come out of great tribulation; they have washed their robes and made them white in the blood of the Lamb.' (Rev.7:9-17)

Bible scholars including this author, consider these people to be tribulation saints as stated in the quote. They are the ones who looked Satan squarely in the eyes said, no, to him and yes to Jesus. Scholars, however, are not unanimous on this. There are those who believe the full Church will go through the *Great Tribulation* and this multitude is the full Church. The weight of biblical scholarship, however, is against this conclusion. The Church will not go through the Great Tribulation. She will be raptured before it starts or at least at the mid-point (3 ½ years in) when suffering and divine judgment are greatly intensified. God's wrath will not be poured out upon His people.

The Day of Salvation

The Church age in which we now live is just about over when the *Rapture* takes place, but the door to salvation will still be slightly opened and millions will squeeze their way through to embrace Jesus Christ as their Savior and Lord, knowing full well this is their last chance. People with a good grasp of eternity will know that the decision made now for hell or heaven, Jesus, or Satan, will be permanent and irrevocable. They are more likely to make the right choice, though it will require much courage to do in the face of certain death. It is in view of these difficult times to come why Christians try hard to win people to Jesus during the day of salvation.

The Church began on the Day of Pentecost with 120 believers in the Upper Room of a private house about AD 33 in First century Jerusalem (Acts 1:120-26, 2:1-7). The Church age is properly ended when Jesus descends from heaven with the Church at the end of the seven years of Great Tribulation (Rav.19:1-21).

CAN I SURVIVE WITHOUT TAKING THE MARK OF THE BEAST?

The Church age is called, the Day of Salvation because it is the time designated for people to come to a salvation experience in Jesus Christ. Except for the seven years of tribulation, it is relatively easy for most people to come Jesus during the Church age. The Bible says, today is the Day of salvation, if you hear the Lord's voice, do not harden your heart as the Israelites did in the wilderness, they resisted God to anger and became the target of His wrath. People are behaving the same way today. And if they live, they will face the wrath of God in a limited way during the Great Tribulation.

It is risky resisting the conviction of the blessed Holy Spirit, leaving your salvation for later; that later may never come for you. The Holy Spirit's mission is to convict people of sin and lead them to Jesus Christ, the only Savior. But the Holy Spirit is not going to hogtie you to bring you to Jesus. He respects your free will. Resisting conviction is dangerous business. A person has the greatest opportunity and advantage to repent of his or her sins now and embrace Jesus as Savior and Lord. You may never have that chance again. If you die physically before the decision is made, you are lost.

Chapter Summary

Let's ask the question again, can a person survive the *Great Tribulation* without taking the *Mark of the Beast*? The honest answer is—your chance of survival is slim to none! I also stated that it is not the right question to ask, and I gave the reasons.

The right question is, will I have the courage to refuse the *Mark of the Beast*? Most people don't know what they will do in a crisis. You may think you are brave and clever now, but when faced with a life-threatening crisis, your response could be quite the opposite. So, rather than planning to be brave and tough, the smart thing to do is plan now not to be here by establishing a right relationship with Jesus Christ. That is your only guarantee of safety. But just in case you find yourself here, the next chapter gives you survival pointers that you must initiate now for time is of the essence.

CHAPTER 5

HOW TO REFUSE THE MARK OF THE BEAST AND SURVIVE

Planning to survive the *Great Tribulation* without taking the *Mark of the Beast* is almost a fool's game and an exercise in futility, but you have a slim chance of succeeding, and so you must try.

The first thing to do when you find out that the Church is gone and you are here, on bended knees, and with a penitent heart invite Jesus Christ into your life. Then resolve that under no circumstances will you take the *Mark of the Beast*. Because if you do take the *Mark of the Beast*, it will be your one-way ticket straight to the eternal flames of hell; you will blow your last chance of making it to heaven. You must convince yourself of that truth and everyone else that joins your team must be so convinced and do the same.

Knowing Jesus Christ as your Savior and Lord is your one-way ticket to eternal life (John 3:16-17). This is no time to debate the fact and truth of this! Make your commitment to Jesus Christ and don't rely on your own strength and cleverness or on your best friend or family, because they will betray you. Know this—even if you survive the *Great Tribulation* without taking the *Mark of the Beast*, you are not out of danger. If you did not commit to Jesus as your Savior and Lord, you must do so to escape hell; eternal life is resident in Jesus Christ alone (John 3:16; Acts 4:12). Freedom is to embrace this truth.

Planning Is Immediate

Chances are—you are reading this book and the *Rapture* has not yet occurred because the Church is still here on earth. There are no broadcast or print media outlets reporting the disappearance of millions of Christians from earth. If the Church is still here, you may still have a little time to carefully think things through and formulate a coherent plan. Of course, there is the danger of slow walking things, thinking you have all the time to play around with.

If the Church is already gone, time is against you! Before you put this book down, start your planning. Since, you cannot survive alone, you must begin to assemble a team of trusted friends and close family members that are in physically good shape, knowledgeable and dependable. This book is teaching you to plan as if the Church is already gone and confusion is everywhere. You and your team must refuse to be confused because this book tells you what has happened and what you must know and do now to survive. From the rapture to the literal, visible return of Jesus to the earth will be seven years. Deception will rule the earth, believe no one, save those on your team. And even with them, keep your eyes wide open.

There will be seven years of suffering such as the world has never seen since the history of humans upon it. The second half of the seven will be most intense and dangerous. You should be safe in your hideout before that. Your plans must be top secret; what you are doing cannot be common knowledge. If every Dick, Tom, Harry, and Susie knows what you are doing, you have already failed before you start. Take time to carefully build a trusted team.

Your Team Is Consisted Of?

A team is like a chain, it is no stronger than its weakest link. One weak personality can betray the whole team. Know the personality of each person on your team. Ask yourself, can this person be trusted, is he or she reliable and dependable, can I trust my life to this person? Does this person talk too much? The point is, choose persons carefully, and don't reveal the full plan until you have the trust of each one.

Remember, Jesus had a team of 12 men He personally picked, and one of them betrayed him. But Jesus knew his betrayer long before Judas carried out the act of betrayal. In other words, even though you develop a level of confidence with these men and women, keep your eyes open, for anyone can betray the team.

Do not choose people on your team for the sake of making up numbers. Each team member should contribute something useful to the team, has a skill that the entire team can benefit from. You are looking for people with survivalist skills, not just book knowledge. A person is strong like an ox, another can swim like a fish, another runs like Husain Bolt; these are good outdoor survivalist skills, don't overlook them. A person may not have technical skills but he or she is a good worker and a good team player; that's a big positive.

Furthermore, a person can learn technical skills over a short period of time. Think of the old TV-show called, the A-Team or the Mission Impossible, each member on the team had a skill. Don't belittle any skill, no matter how simple. You will find good use for it.

This book is not the Bible; it is a guide! So be creative, build a team with what you have. I am sharing with you what the ideal team looks like, but very few teams will meet this ideal, that's okay! The ideal team will have people with skills, some of these categories:

1. *Survivalist skills*: this person knows how to live outdoors, live off the land, how to start a fire without matches, hunt game,

fish without traditional fishing equipment, survive in a snow cave, knows how to swim, dive, build a raff out of logs, even a canoe, if needed. Make water pipes with bamboo. These skills are important because cities will not make for good hideouts; remote, deep wilderness, away from civilization is best.

2. *Communication Experts*: this person knows how to use a satellite phone, knows how to make regular cell phone calls untraceable, generate electricity from solar energy, knows how to intercept communication, knows something about cyber security encryption, knows how to operate a ham radio, has computer skills, including software skills.

3. *Security skills*: knows how to handle weapon of different type, knows self-defense. This person is perhaps an x-police or security guard, serves in the arm forces, knows how to do surveillance, fly a done for photographic surveillance.

4. *Construction Skills*: Basic knowledge and Skills should include: the ability to read blueprint/schematic drawing and to make them for any project (able to read measurements and do basic calculations), knowledge of brick laying, carpentry, plumbing, electrical work, concrete work, working with wood, stones, roofing. Knowledge of equipment for these categories including electric generators, solar panels. Outdoors/indoors

tools: saw, hammer, nails, plyers, wrenches, screw drivers, picks shovels, axe, cutlas (machete).

5. *Leadership skills*: Every group need a leader who can think critically, makes decisive decisions, knows how to delegate responsibility, knows how to listen, to encourage, and so on.

6. *Healthcare Skills*: basic knowledge of medication, first aid, nursing, EMS work, Heimlich maneuver, administer CPR, stop bleeding, dress a wound, set a broken hand or leg, administers, and oversees first aid supplies, secure medications.

7. *Home or Institution (hotel, assisted living) management skills: Basic* Knowledge of meal preparation, knowledge of food storage management and supplies, and ensure that the group does not run out of food. Knowledge of food safety. Basic *housekeeping skills:* knowledge of how to manage living quarters for safety, hygiene, sanitation, garbage, clothing, and toiletries.

8. *Water Specialist Knowledge and Skills:* Able to turn water from any source into safe drinking water: sea water, pond water, unclean river water, unsafe well-water, snow water, even drill for water if necessary. Knows how to chemically treat water or sterilize it by boiling before drinking.

9. *Spiritual Leadership Skills*: Knowledgeable of the Bible, how to pray, counsel, teach, provide spiritual guidance. At the beginning, some team members will have to be convinced of what's written in this book and the Bible itself. This person must teach the team, that they can know what is happening in the world and what is going to happen, and how to prepare for it. Have Bible study, time for prayer and so on.

General and Sub-teams:

Your general team is all the people with you; they form your community. Use the skill stated in the preceding section to arrange community members into sub-teams of about 3 or 4 per team. The size of each sub-teams depends on the size of the community. The community is the pool from which you draw sub-team members. You can use that same skills list to screen new members coming into the community. This gives you a firsthand idea of the skills they have.

The leader will arranger the general community into sub-teams according to skills, ability, and work responsibilities. This section gives examples of your sub-teams of 3 to 4 members each. They must be self-sufficient as possible. One person on each team serves as the leader of that team. The leader is not a boss, all members are working together but they are accountable to the leader who in turn is accountable to the director of the community.

The following sub-teams are suggested:

1. Leadership Team (3-4 Persons):

a) *Qualifications:* This team is consisted of the director of the community, the assistant director, the secretary, and the spiritual leader. They should have leadership skills that include decisiveness, calm, positive attitude, fairness, able to listen, able to think analytically, understand human personality, able to conduct a meeting. *Secretary:* Good writing skill, knowledge of computer word processing, good reader. *Spiritual leader:* good knowledge of the Bible, knows how to pray, able to understand this book and explain it others.

b) *Functions:* The *Director* is the head authority of the community. He or she leads the community, supervises all teams, move around personnel, assign responsibilities, provide counsel and discipline. The *Assistant* provides support to the director and is in charge if the director is unable to function. The *secretary* documents the day-to-day happenings of the community, take minutes of all official meetings, preserve all records. The *Spiritual Leader* is responsible for the spiritual life of the community: worship, prayer, bible study, baptism, counseling, funerals, and marriages.

2. **Constructions team (3-4 members):**

   a) *Qualifications*--the members of this sub-team have basic knowledge and skills to read and make blueprint or schematic drawing, understand basic measurement or calculations, basic knowledge of construction: brick laying, carpentry, plumbing, electrical, concrete work, working with wood, stones, roofing.

   b) *They have basic* knowledge of the equipment and tools to get the work done in skill's categories for their area, including electric generators, solar panels. Outdoors-indoors tools: saw, hammer, nails, plyers, wrenches, screw drivers, picks shovels, axe, cutlas (machete).

   c) Responsible for all the tools and equipment assigned to their sub-team.

   d) Function: Once the living location is identified and agreed upon, the team will do the construction work, safe and suitable to accommodate the community.

3. ***Communication & Navigation Team:***

a) *Qualifications*: this team understands how to get around undetected by air, land, and water, knows compass reading, map reading, global positioning, computer knowledge, cyber knowledge include encryption skills (able to access the Internet undetected). Use of satellite phone, understanding of satellite positioning, drone piloting and surveillances photographing.
b) This team is responsible for all communication to and from the community; it keeps custody of all devices used for communication. Ensures that all communication is encrypted, untraceable, and hacker proof. It confiscates all unauthorized communication devices. It briefs the community on important outside happenings.
c) It charts the navigation route of the community or anyone sent out on mission or reconnaissance.

4. *Health team* (2-3 persons):

a) Qualifications: At least one or more persons must be a medical doctor or a Registered Nurse or a License Practical Nurse or an EMS person, and or a trained Home Health Aide.
b) Function: Their function of is to provide appropriate healthcare services for all members of the community,

secure all medical instruments and medication; administer first aid.

c) To certify deaths, if any.

5. *House Management team (3-4 persons):*

a) Qualification: Knowledge of running a family home, adult home, hotel, motel, knowledge of meal preparation, food management and safety.

b) Function: manage the living quarters. See that quarters are kept clean, Prepare meals, store food and supplies, care of toiletry supply, and laundry.

6. *Water safety & sanitation Team* (2-3 persons):

a) *Qualification*: Basis knowledge of water purification and sanitation. Able to turn any kind of water into safe drinking water, able to locate water in the ground. Know to keep drinking water separate from sanitation water.

b) *Provide safe drinking water, water domestic use, safe disposal of sanitation water.*

7. *Security & Safety team* (3-4 Persons):

a) Qualifications: basic knowledge of environmental security, home and business security, weapons security and use, self-defense, cyber security.
b) Protect the community from outside intruders, ensures that no community member compromises the security of the community by leaving the community or unauthorized contact to the outside. Security and safety of course is everybody's business, if you see something, say something or do something.

8. ***Mechanic Team***:
    a) *Qualifications*: basic knowledge of all aspects of automotive repairs, electrical motors, and generators.
    b) *Function*: render functional all engines and electrical motors that were heretofore dysfunctional or partly defective.

THE HIDING PLACE

Since no one can safely hide out at his or her usual home, a hideout must be carefully chosen. It cannot be a place that has the likelihood of being discovered. It must be extremely remote. The knowledge of its location is top secret; No more than 3 to 4 persons need to know the location before occupancy, preferrable from the leadership team.

A Secure Hiding Place

First, the team becomes a family, and as painful as it may be, you will need to sever ties with blood family and friends who are not a part of this group. Any team member who contacts or visits family is at risk of betraying the whole team, wittingly or unwittingly.

Perhaps, a tropical or semi-tropical place like California, Arizona, Nevada, or a Caribbean Island would be Ideal. Preferrable, a mountainous place like Jamaica, with deep woodlands, caves, streams, and very remote. It should be a region people are not usually found. It will be unwise to travel to another country to a hideout because, international travel will most certainly reveal a person's identity.

The ideal is to have three locations that are miles apart, and you can get from one to the other without being seen. If one location is suspected of being compromised, the community can move to another. The group must be prepared to travel from one hideout to another in a moment's notice. If the locations are in the snowbelt, special thought and planning must be given to the winter months and the extreme heat of summer. Some heaters give off carbon dioxide or monoxide that can kill the whole community. Be careful.

All three hideouts will have to be carefully fortified and supplied with all survival necessities months or years before they are needed. This means funds will have to be collected over time to finance the project including hideout A, B, and C. Again, three locations are the ideal, perhaps, your group can only do one.

If your hideout is a cave, be sure it is not flooded when it rains or when snow melts. A cave will require some work to convert it to safe and comfortable living space. If the region has snakes, it should be thoroughly searched for them. Other animals will be less threatening unless there are mountain lions and animals of suck kind.

The security team may confer with the construction team concerning the creation of a holding or confinement cell in the hideout in case the community must deal with a worst-case scenario. The likelihood of it being used is small, but it could be the answer for worst-case situations. For example, holding a person discovered to have the *Mark of the Beast* as opposed to dismissing or executing him. Release the person at the end of the hideout, not before.

In choosing a hiding place, give critical thought to water accessibility. If there is no water source nearby, do you have the skills on your team to create your own? With the proper knowledge, any water can be converted to safe drinking water, if you have a source.

The Hiding Place Administration

HOW TO REFUSE THE MARK OF THE BEAST AND SURVIVE

This hideout community serves as its own government. The leader will have the whole team elect members to a Judicial Council that decides critical decision such as admitting certain people to the hideout or depriving a person of his or her freedom if they become a threat to the community. Dismissing a person from the community will be difficult because that person will reveal the hiding place.

The leadership team over time should put together a set of By-laws that the whole community adopts and live by. The leadership team with 3 additional members at large chosen by the community could function as the *Judicial Council* (a type of court). It is a separate body and meets at most twice a year but can call emergency meetings as needed. For example, if someone stole away from the community and was compromised such as taking the *Mark of the Beat,* what should the community do? Of course, this would be a worst-case scenario. The Judicial Council will have to condemn that person to life confinement, death or expel from the community? No easy choice! He or she belongs to Satan and will hand over the community at the opportune time. The Judicial Council must decide what to do with this person to save the community.

The leadership team, spoken of earlier administers the bylaws that guide the community. The hideout is designed to house a limited number of persons, but in the first 3 years, if there is space, a member of the team can recommend family members or friend to be considered for admission; the leadership will screen the person away from the hideout. A person with the *Mark of the Beast* cannot be accepted to the community or someone who is so physically compromised, they just use up the resources of the community.

No personal cell phone is allowed in the community, phones must be destroyed, surrendered voluntarily, or confiscated by security. Additionally, no individual is allowed to make contact to the outside world since calls can be traced back to the hideout location and endanger the whole community. One satellite phone is allowed to the community, held by the communication's expert who may place any necessary calls on behalf of community members.

A team of 3 to 5 can do deep woods farming to supply the community with fresh vegetables of different kinds. This farming is done in small gardens at a distance from the hideout so it does not give away the *hideou*t to any outside persons who may stumble on the garden.

The garden or gardens must be done in such a way that they blend in with the natural surroundings. So, avoid clearing large area as people usually do for farming. Just clear several six-inch locations in the forest where sunlight is accessible, each is enough to hold one head of cabbage or lettuce, or pepper plant, pumpkin or cucumber or string beans and so on. One could be standing in such garden and don't know it. Neither can it be spotted from a far by someone who does not know it is there.

Always be quiet when visiting garden, observe garden and surrounding areas with binoculars from a distance for about 30 minutes before planting, caring for, or reaping. Do not bring any identifying information that will lead anyone to the hideout. Carry a compass and if discovered do not run back to the hideout but away from it until it is certain that you lose the strangers, you may return quietly to the hideout.

Learn how to make fire without smoke. Smoke can be picked up from the air by aircraft and give away the hiding place. Always be security conscious and quiet, always wear camouflage clothing that blend in with the natural environment. Be aware of smoking of tobacco or any other weeds that gives off a fragrance to alert an intruder that someone is in the area.

It is good when moving through the forest to have a double-barrel rifle, the kind that is used for hunting, have a hunting shoulder back. In case you stumble on anyone from who you cannot hide. Have a story, a false name, a town where you are from, you are bird hunting. Get as much information as you can without giving any. Do not engage in any conversation about government. If they look frightened, tell them they should not be seen in these woods again.

Caught on a Mission

If you are caught while on a mission for the community, what do you do? First, chances are words will get back to the community urgently, because, in most cases, no person would be on a solo mission for the community; in such case, your partner will undoubtedly alert the community of your capture. But if your partner is also caught, the community will have to figure out that you are captured.

If you are being chased, never run back directly to the community; in such case, you would be leading them directly to the hideout. In like manner, if you suspect that you are being watched and followed, never come straight back to the community. Remember, you only have two loyalties: God and the community. Your loyalty to God is that under no circumstances will you take the *Mark of the Beast,* if you do take it, you are eternally damned. If you don't, your captors will execute you but your life is safe in the Lord.

Second, under no circumstance should you give any information about the community. You may be tortured and under the sentence of death. But nothing they do to you can be worse than hell. You see, if you cooperate with them, they may let you live, but they will not let you go without attaching to you the *Mark of the Beast.* And with that *Mark* you are as good as dead, Satan owns you and you will spend your eternity with him in the lake of burning sulfur or hell (Rev.20:7-10, 15).

CHAPTER 6
WILL RAPTURED BELIEVERS RETURN TO EARTH?

You may have family members and friends that went to heaven in the rapture (they were taken up alive), and you are wondering what are they doing, will they return to earth, and when? This chapter will briefly answer these questions. For more extensive discussion see my book, *The Book of Life & The Books of Wrath*.

Anatomical Constitutional Change

The first thing to remember is the fact that all the persons taken up to heaven alive, went through a physical change of their bodies. The physical body was not designed to live in heaven, even astronauts going to space must have a space suit designed for that environment. The third heaven where God dwells is where believers go at the time of the Rapture; it much farther away than where astronauts go. It is perhaps many light-years away. A light-year is the distance that light travels in one year, moving at a speed of 186,000 miles per second. Human physical body was not designed to live in that celestial environment, that is why the Bible tells us flesh and blood cannot "inherit eternal life" (1 Cor.15:50).

For this reason, Raptured believers will undergo immediate physical body change before leaving the earth's atmosphere. The apostle Paul speaks of this change, "We will not all sleep, but we will all be changed. For the perishable must clothe itself with the imperishable, and the mortal with immortality…" (15: 51-53; 1 Thes.4:16-17).

So, all believers, those that died in the Lord and those are alive and in Christ, will all get a new body that can live anywhere, heaven or earth (2 Cor.5:1-5). It will be a body like unto the glorious resurrection body of our Lord Jesus Christ. Paul speaks of this in Philippians 3: 20-21: "But our citizenship is in heaven. And we eagerly await a Savior from there, the Lord Jesus Christ, who, by the power that enables him to bring everything under his control, will transform our lowly bodies so that they will be like his glorious body" (Philip.3:20-21). The apostle John also speaks of this transformation in 1John 3:2-3. So, bear in mind that they were raptured to heaven are now living in a body that dies no more, and it capable of living on earth and in heaven. Those who are left on earth are still in a physical body; they can die by someone killing them or by accident or by disease, even though they may have made Jesus their Lord and Savior.

What are they Doing in Heaven?

First, they will face judgment. This is called, the believers' judgment. Paul, the apostle, speaks of it in these words, "For we must all appear before the judgment seat of Christ, so that each of us may receive what is due us for the things done while in the body whether good or bad" (2 Cor.5:10). Note, that this is inclusive judicial lingual, "We must all appear." It's as if you have a subpoena to appear in court." This is called, the believers judgment because no unbeliever will be here; they have their own judgment, and they will know when and where they must appear (Rev.20:11-15).

The purpose of the believers' judgment is not to judge them for sins; believers' sins are forgiven; God keeps no record them. Our sins were placed of Jesus Christ, and He paid the full penalty for them on the cross; He took our place (Isa.53:3-11; Rom.5:1-7,19). If somebody pays your debt, legally you don't owe that debt anymore; you can't face judgment twice for the same offence. No believer will be turned out of heaven because of this judgment.

Second, they will be receiving their reward. The purpose of the *believers' judgment* is to review and reward believers for the work they did for Jesus Christ since the day they accepted Him as Savior and Lord. Don't get me wrong, it will be a tough judgment with tears and regrets, but no one will be thrown out. Some believers will get no reward, because they were lazy Christians, they did little or nothing for the Lord. There are other believers who have worked hard for the Lord and will receive no reward because they did not do their work out of love for the Lord; they did it for money and the glory of self (that was their reward – Matthew 6:1-6).

Believers' work will be tried by the fire of judgment and the fire will destroy works that were not rendered in love, and no reward will be issued for those works (1 Cor.3:6-15). Faithful believers will be rewarded. Paul talks about a crown of life that the Lord, the righteous Judge, will reward him and other faithful believers on that day (2 Tim.4:6-8). For more details on the Believers Judgment, see *The Book of Life & The Books* by this author.

Third, they will be attending the Marriage Supper of the Lamb. The Church is called the Bride of Christ and Jesus is referred to as the bridegroom. This is a figure of speech denoting that the Church will be permanently united to Jesus Christ. The only union on earth that faintly describes this closeness and celebration is a marriage.

WILL RAPTURED BELIEVERS RETURN TO EARTH?

The scripture adopts the language of marriage to describe this unique, heavenly celebration (Eph.5:21-33; Rev.19:1-9).

Note, Church members are not going to be angel; angels are a different class of Beings. We are not going to be bodyless ghosts. We will be glorified humans in a body designed to live anywhere, eat and drink without getting fat, diseased sickness or death. Those who miss the Rapture will surely miss a lot. The Word of God declares, "Blessed are those who are invited to the wedding supper of the Lamb!" (Rev.19:9 NIV). Every born-again believer, living a holy and obedient life in Jesus Christ is invited. The scripture is clear, the wedding takes place in heaven and a great multitude attend (Rev.1-9).

The Church Returns with Jesus

Jesus will return to earth after the marriage supper of the Lamb, and at the end of the seven years tribulation. In fact, His return to earth with His Church will bring the Great Tribulation to an end.

But *The Great Tribulation* will not end in a whimper; it will end in a World War. Historically, Satan's aim is to wipe Israel off the face of the earth. He has tried many times without success; his most valiant try was Hitler's holocaust and he failed. For the first time Satan has command of the collective arm forces of the world and the world of humankind. He will now set his sights on national Israel which is about mid-point of the Great Tribulation.

Remember, when the Beast first emerge on the global stage, he comes as a man of peace, offering solutions to global problems and crises, including the Arab Israeli conflict. To get Israel on board, this global leader will make an offer too good to refuse, perhaps security accommodation in the form of a peace treaty. But this treaty is a deception. The favored, generous terms of the treaty will lead Israel to think the deceiver is their long-awaited Messiah.

But 3 ½ years later, the Beast will break the treaty with Israel (Dan.9:27). It happens, perhaps, when the second Beast of Revelation 13 arrive and begin to enforce the policies of the Antichrist's without exception. He builds a talking image and installs it in all places of worship worldwide and begin to force people to worship it or die.

To Jews and Christians, this is sacrilegious and blasphemous. The Jewish and Christian Scriptures said, Hear Oh, Israel the LORD your God, the LORD is One. You shall not make for yourselves any carved image, you shall not bow down to them nor serve them, I am the LORD! (Exodus 20:1-6; Deut.5:7-10). Since the true Church is already gone from the earth, Jews will be left totally defenseless.

Jews will wake up to the fact that they have been deceived, that this is another Hitler. They will vigorously refuse to be marked by this devil and they will not throw the Torah in the trash and worship him. They will mount a resistance against the Antichrist government and Jews will be slaughtered.

WILL RAPTURED BELIEVERS RETURN TO EARTH?

The antichrist will marshal his military forces to invade Jerusalem to wipe Israel off the face of the earth. But just before military orders to exterminate Jews and Jerusalem are executed, trumpets sound in the heavens, Jesus, the true Messiah appears in the clouds of glory leading an army of saints and angels. The apostle John describes the scene for us:

> I saw heaven standing open and there before me a white horse, whose rider is called Faithful and True. With justice he judges, and wages war. His eyes are like blazing fire, and on his head are many crowns. He has a name written on him, that no one knows but he himself. He is dressed in a robe dipped in blood, and his name is the Word of God. The armies of heaven are following him, riding on white horses and dressed in fine linen, white and clean. Coming out of his mouth is a sharp sword with which he strikes down the nations. He will rule them with an iron scepter. He treads the winepress of the fury of the wrath of God. On his robe and on his thigh, he has this name written: KING OF KINGS AND LORD OF LORDS. (Rev,19:11-16)

This is no Gulf War I and II with coalition of nations in the Middle East. This is much bigger! This is a gathering of the armies of all the nations of earth to fight Jesus and the armies of heaven. This is the best of earth's military might against the Almighty. How can mortals fight immortals and win? The show down is referred to as "Armageddon."

Before the war starts, arrangements are made by a mighty angel to assemble a vast cleanup crew of vultures to devour dead bodies after the war. The apostle John gives us a picture of this arrangement: "And I saw an angel standing in the sun, who cried in a loud voice to all the birds flying in midair, 'Come, gather together for the great supper of God, so that you may eat the flesh of kings, generals, and the mighty, of horses and their riders, and the flesh of all people, free and slaves, great and small'"(Rev.19:17-18 NIV). The apostle John goes on to describe the war and records the outcome of a war which is Still in the future:

> Then I saw the beast and the kings of the earth and their armies gathered together to wage war against the rider on the horse and his army. But the beast was captured, and with it the false prophet who had performed signs on his behalf. With these signs he had deluded those who had received the mark of the beast and worship his image. The two of them were thrown alive into the fiery lake of burning sulfur. The rest were killed with the sword coming out of the mouth of the rider on the horse, and all the birds gorged themselves on their flesh. (Rev.19:19-21)

WILL RAPTURED BELIEVERS RETURN TO EARTH?

Jesus upon His arrival captures the Antichrist and the False prophet, Satan's leading executives, and they are both thrown into the lake of burning sulfur as the preceding quote indicates. Jesus then issues an order to capture Satan; he is captured and placed into prison (Rev.20:1-3). The capture of Satan does not require an army of angels, one mighty angel is more than able to do the job.

Jesus and His Church will then march into Jerusalem where Jesus will sit upon the throne of David and rule over the earth in peace for a thousand years (Isa.9:6-7). This is called, the millennium. His followers will be appointed to rule as kings, governors, and mayors over different cities across the world.

No sooner than the war ends, *left-behinders* can exit their hideout. You can now rebuild your life in the new world order; conditions will more favorable that before. There will be peace and prosperity everywhere. Of course, you will be a subject of the government of Jesus Christ. Life will be good, but some dangers still exist. You will be in the same physical body whereas many of those you will now interact with will be in bodies far superior to yours.

In as much as Satan is in prison, he still has followers that will be loyal to him. You make sure that you are loyal to Jesus Christ. Some, if not most, of these loyalists will be people born during the millennium. You have survived the *Great Tribulation* without taking the Mark of the Beast. But you have missed out on a whole lot.

Had you accepted Jesus and went to heaven and returned with Jesus as part of the raptured body of believers, you would have had a new body not subject to disease or death, and you would be either, king, governor, or mayor over some city. You won't go to hell if you stay loyal to Jesus. But you will grow old and die, but at the end of the millennium you will be resurrected and given the same status as us, a new body that dies no more.

The wicked will be resurrected and judged and thrown into hell with Satan at the end of the millennium (Rev.20:7-15). People who are born in the millennium and rejected Jesus, will face judgment in their physical body. They will be sentenced to the lake of burning sulfur. God is big on love and mercy, but He is also the God of justice. Do not fool yourself in thinking everybody is going to be saved.

CHAPTER 7
Kingdom Age BEGINS

The Church age officially ends with the return of Jesus Christ with the Church to earth from heaven. With that the rule of human government comes to an end, and Satan's reign comes to an end. Of course, Satan is not yet thrown into the lake of burning sulfur or hell. This will happen sometime later in accordance with God's time. Perhaps, Satan has unfinished business to attend to. It is God who determines his end, for in some strange way, Satan serves the purpose of God.

However, Satan will not be allowed to roam the earth doing his usual mischief at this time; he will be in prison (Rev.20:1-3).

What is kingdom age, how long will it last, what will life be like upon the earth, what will happen when it ends? This chapter will briefly answer these questions. For more extensive discussion, I refer you to my book, *The Book of Life & The Books of Wrath*.

What is Kingdom Age?

Kingdom Age is a period of one thousand years, running from the second advent of Jesus to this earth and ends with the final Judgment (Rev.19:11-20:1-15). Jesus will be literally sitting on the throne of King David and rule over the earth from Israel's Capital city, Jerusalem. Jerusalem has been the capital from the time of King David and will always be, though for political correctness, it is not recognized as such internationally. But in the heart of every true Jew, it is, and by the time of Jesus' second advent, it will be recognized as such.

Christians have always recognized Jesus Christ as Prophet, Priest, and King. His prophetic role is designated as the time of His ministry on earth during His first advent. According to the book of Hebrews, Jesus is now performing His High Priestly role in heaven. He will return to earth to reign as King of king and Lord of lords (Rev.19:16). He returns to reign!

From ancient times, several Hebrew prophets speak of this time when the Messiah will reign as Israel's king from Jerusalem. Most of those prophets did not understand that there would have been a first coming and a second coming of the Messiah with the Church age sandwiched in between, a time of salvation from sin for Israel and the world. They just saw the Messiah coming as a mighty deliverer for Israel much like Moses who liberated them from Egypt.

KINGDOM AGE BEGINS

The prophet Isaiah for example, gives us this wonderful passage concerning the Messiah's reign:

> For unto us a child is born, unto us a son is given: and the government shall be upon his shoulder and his name shall be called, Wonderful, Counsellor, The might God, The everlasting Father, The Prince of Peace. Of the increase of his government and peace there shall be no end, upon the throne of David, and upon his kingdom, to order it with judgment and with justice from henceforth even forever. The zeal of the LORD of hosts will perform this. (Isiah 9:6-7 KJV)

Isaiah gave this prophecy 700 years before the first coming of Jesus Christ as a baby born in a manger in Bethlehem, but the prophecy is not fulfilled until the second Advent of Jesus Christ. Jesus did not sit on any throne of government and rule over the world at His first coming, but He will upon returning. And the time of His reign is referred to as Kingdom Age or the Millennium, which means a thousand (Rev.20:1-7).

You could understand why the Jews were looking to Jesus at His first coming to throw off the Roman occupation and restore their nation's pride to the golden years of King David and King Solomon. They didn't even know that there was going to be a second coming of the Messiah, and for them to accept Yeshua (Jesus) as their Messiah

He must do what they expected a Messiah to do, liberate Israel. Did Jesus make any attempt to do that? No! Not in a physical sense.

Had Jesus shown any political, revolutionary interest, they would have crowned Him as their long-awaited Messiah. Jesus had no interest in opposing or unseating Caesar at that time. Frankly, He was more friendly to Caesar's government and more eager to pay taxes than the average Jew. Jesus even added a tax-collector to his ministry team and went to their homes to have meals as it was in the case of Zacchaeus (Luke 19:1-10). Such behaviors did not sit well with the Jewish authorities. Tax collectors were generally Jews who collected Caesar's taxes, and thy were hated by their fellow Jews.

Jesus kept talking about the kingdom of heaven, but when pressed about this kingdom, he said it was not of this world. He refused to be king on their terms, and with that he became a threat and an imposter to them, so they had him crucified. When you understand the Hebrew's mindset here, you see the motivation of the disciple's frequent question to Jesus concerning the restoration of the Davidic kingdom to Israel. They asked this question up to the very day Jesus ascended to heaven (Acts 1:3-11).

Like national Israel, the disciples at first, failed to understand the redemptive nature of Jesus' mission. They did not see or understand the connection to the Church Age, the preaching of the gospel, and the foundational role they would play in that enterprise until the blessed Holy Spirit came. The fog began to clear.

With the coming of the Holy Spirit on the Day of Pentecost, they began to understand the spiritual aspect of the kingdom (Acts 2). The ministry of the apostle Paul brought further revelation, clarifying the true nature, extent, and purpose of the Church age, that both Gentiles and Jews would form one Body in Christ (Eph.2:11-22; Gal.1-2; Col.1:14-29). Paul appears to have had a fuller understanding of the Church and its mission before the other apostles, even though they were apostles before him (Gal.1:8-2:2). No wonder he worked so hard and wrote so much.

The redemptive, spiritual aspect of the kingdom precedes the literal coming of the kingdom. The visible aspect of the kingdom with Jesus sitting on the throne of David is at the end of the Church age. In the Church age, God is establishing His rule in the hearts of humankind. That is why Jesus, on one hand said, "The Kingdom of God is in you" ( ). Yet, on the other hand he said, pray for the kingdom to come (Matt.6:9-10).

The Nature of Kingdom Age

What will the kingdom age be like? Frankly, many Christians don't even know there will be such a thing as *Kingdom Age.* Other than people and things around us getting old, we don't normal think of times in terms of age. But that's how Bible writers conceived of long period of time in which God deals with humans. They talk about ages past, the present age, and the ages to come. "Oh God, our help in ages past, our hope for years to come," the hymn says.

During the Kingdom age, Jesus Christ is not only ruling in the hearts of humankind; He is also reigning as the visible head of worldwide government. As Isaiah said, "the government will be upon his shoulders" (Isa.9:6 NIV). Here is the thing, Satan knows the Kingly rule of Jesus is coming and tries to offer that position easily to Him without the pain of the cross. All Jesus had to do in exchange is to worship Satan (Matt.4: 8-10). Satan's attempt is audacious!

Of course, if Jesus accepted Satan's off, that includes Jesus sidestepping the cross, so there would be no redemption for humankind. The human family would fully become Satan's family. But that's not all—it would also create a fracture in the Godhead. This would be a greater mess than the one made by Adam and Eve when they accepted Satan's suggestion. When his trick to deceive Jesus failed, Satan tried others including crucifixion, but Jesus overcome death by resurrection and returned to heaven with the promise to return (John 14:1-4 ; Acts 1:9-11).

The One-world government with Satan and his two sidekicks (the antichrist, and the False prophet), spoken of earlier, is Satan's pre-emptive move to setup his own government over the earth to prevent Jesus from returning as King over the world.

To pull this off, Satan established himself as a false trinity: Satan himself imitating God the Father, the Antichrist imitating God the Son, and the False prophet imitating God the Holy Spirit. But his brutal imitation government is brought to it end when Jesus descended from heaven with an army of saints and angels and crushed them with a sharp sword from His mouth. The sword is His Word; he speaks, and they die (Rev.19:15). The Antichrist and the False prophet are captured and thrown into hell alive; Satan is arrested and chained in the abyss (Rev.19:19-21, 20:1-3).

Satan was bold enough to lead a third of heaven's angels in an insurrection to dethrone God, but he failed in that endeavor (Rev.12:7-10). Now, he has led billions of human beings with the collective war machines of earth to take a stand to prevent Jesus from coming to rule as King over the earth. He has failed this one too; he is now in prison as we have seen earlier.

In case you have not noticed, this is about the fourth big defeat Satan has suffered from the Lord: 1) defeated in his uprising in heaven (Rev.12:7-10), 2) defeated in his wilderness temptation of Jesus (Matt.4:1-11), 3) defeated by the cross and resurrection of Jesus (Gen.3:15;Heb.2:14;Rev.1:18), 4) again defeated upon Jesus' arrival at the end of the *Great Tribulation* (Rev.19:19-20:1-3, 8-10). He is finally thrown into the eternal lake of burning sulfur, commonly referred to as hell; that is the place he belongs.

The Government of Jesus

Now that Jesus has finally defeated His archenemy, destroyed his war machine, vanquished Satan's human followers, and has rid the earth of them all—what will Jesus' government be like? We will try to answer this question briefly in this section.

First, the government of Jesus Christ (of God) is not a democracy. It looks like a monarchy because Jesus is King over all the earth. He is not elected or appointed to this position by any human or created being. So, it is a true theocracy, a government under God.

Satan is called a thief and a liar, a usurper. He wants his own kingdom, so he seized earth from Adam, made himself god over it, and during the *Great Tribulation* he seeks to make it a kingdom under Satan. But from early in the biblical narrative, we read that the Kingdom belongs to God (Ps.2, 22:28). Jesus wants us to remind Satan that the kingdom and its glory belong to God by making that affirmation to God when we pray (Matt.6:13). We should also pray for the kingdom of God to come to earth (vv.9-10).

Second, believers will be ruling over this earthly kingdom with Jesus. Jesus is the *only begotten Son of God* (John 3:16). But believers are called, "hairs of God and joint-hairs" with Jesus. We are "children of God" by spiritual birth and by adoption (Rom.14-17).

If God is our Father as we are taught in the Lord's Prayer and throughout scripture, then we share in the inheritance of our Father. Jesus speaks of the kingdom inheritance reality in these words:

> For all the nations of this world seek after these things and your Father knows that you need them. Instead, seek his kingdom, and these things will be added to you. Fear not little flock, for it is your Father's good pleasure to give you the kingdom. (Luke 12:30-32 ESV)

On another occasion Jesus said to His disciples, "You are those who have stayed with me in my trials, and I assign to you, as my Father assigned to me a kingdom, that you may eat and drink at my table in my kingdom and sit on thrones judging the twelve tribes of Israel" (Luke 22:28-30 ESV). So, believers will rule as kings, governors, and lords over the nations and cities of the earth under Jesus who is THE KING of king and LORD of Lords (Rev.19:16).

Third, all kings and lords ruling under Jesus are in glorified bodies. They don't get sick and die and you cannot outwit them.

Fourth, there will be global peace and unprecedented prosperity, such as the world has never seen since the Fall of man.

Fifth, people will work, raise a family, worship, obey authorities, give out their full age, die as we do now. But life will not be as difficult, sickly, stressful, worrisome as it is now. Life will be gloriously happy worldwide. People will get married, babies born, grow up and will accept or reject Jesus as we do now. People will not be forced to accept Jesus. Perhaps, that's why Satan will be let out of prison for a short time to tie up loose ends will his followers.

Sixth, evil will be at a bare minimum for Satan will be in prison for the full length of the kingdom age, one thousand years (Rev.20:1-3). Sin will still be in the heart of those who are not yet glorified. Some of them will be diehard Satan followers that will keep his enterprise alive while he is in prison. That is why Satan will be paroled for a short time. He will reassembly his followers to make one last assault on Jesus. All his human followers will be destroyed, and Satan finally thrown into hell (vv.7-10).

Seventh, Kingdom age ends with the Final Judgment. Satan is thrown into hell, the wicked dead are resurrected, judged, and thrown into hell, and all living humans who have rejected Jesus Christ will be judged and thrown into hell. The earth will either be destroyed or renovated by fire, and there will be a new heaven and a new earth, the new Jerusalem its eternal capital. It will be a completely new world order where dwells righteousness. Much of what will be is classified, known only to the blessed Holy Trinity.

APPENDIX A

YOUR QUALITY OF LIFE IN HIDING

Introduction

God has given you the right to life and the pursuit of happiness, not even the devil in hell himself can be allowed to take this from you. Don't allow him; don't give him a chance to rob you of your freedom. You may be hiding in a cave in some remote place, but you are not an animal, and you must refuse to live like one. You are the image bearer of God; you have supreme worth and value to Him. And in all things, He is the one you seek to please above all else. Live your life joyfully!

To do well physically and mentally, you should get up each day, not anxiously focused on hiding or wringing your hands in quiet desperation, hoping your hiding place is not discovered. The Word of God warns against such anxiety because it is unhealthy and not consistent with the life of faith (Matt.6: 25-34).Yes, you need to be careful and smart. But to do that, you must preserve your mental health, your physical health, your spiritual health, and avoid destructive conflict. These four things.

For these four things to be realized in the community by each member, you must individually and collectively care for each other and not unduly get on a person's nerves. Avoid little cliques forming against each other. Remember, the goal is for each community member is to get through this alive and well and without the *Mark of the Beast*. That is the survival mission that you must not lose vision of. But in the meantime, cultivate and practice a healthy lifestyle.

For the community to achieve the four stated health goals (mental, physical, spiritual, and relational health) members cannot just get up and sitting around each day in distress about when this is going to be over. If you do that, your health on all four levels will quickly deteriorate and you will all go crazy destroying each other.

To achieve the best and avoid the worst, the following daily routine is suggested for the whole community. You may adopt the schedule as written or adjust it to suit your community's situation. Your schedule includes uniform bedtime, uniform rising time, breakfast time, worship time, work time, day of rest, exercise time, games time, group time, worship time, entertainment time.

APPENDIX A

Suggested Community Routine

Workdays: Mon-Fri. 9-5, Sat. 9-12 Sunday: Rest Day

Bedtime……………………11:00 pm (weekdays): Lights off, community retires for bed, 2-night guards on duty.

Wake time………………5-6:00 a.m. (Awake, personal prayer, use of shower).

Breakfast time………… 7-8:00 am: Communal breakfast

Worship…………………..8:05-8:30: Singing, prayer, scripture, exhortation

Work time………………9-5:00 Team about their assigned duties, security patrols, and do surveillance.

Lunch Time……………12-1:00 pm

Dinner Time…………..6-7:30 PM

Sunday Schedule

- *Breakfast: 8:00 AM*
- *Morning Worship: 10:00 AM*
- *Dinner Time: 5:00 PM*

Physical & Mental Health

Physical and mental health are inextricable connected. When you physically exercise, it also helps your mental health. Exercise a minimum of three days a week, one hour each time (3 times per week, 1 hour each). If the community has over 28 members, divide the community into 3 groups (group 1, 2, 3):

- Group 1 Mondays 5: 00 am. Wed. 7:30Pm, Fri.7:30 PM
- Group 2 Tuesdays 5:00 am. Thur. 7:30 PM, Sat. 7:30 am
- Group 3 Wednesdays 5:00 am, Fri.8:30 PM, Sun.6:00 am
- For 28 members or less, you can divide into 2 groups or meet as one group.

Friday Night: Entertainment Night 8-12 PM

- *Comedy*
- *Solo, duet, Quartet*
- *Story telling*
- *Self-defense*
- *Games*

Saturday Morning Group (8-10 a.m.):

Your spiritual health is also nurtured through your quiet prayer life with God, communal prayer, study of God's word, worship, breaking of bread. These times set aside are very important and you should not miss them. Without them you could wither on the vine and die spiritually (John 15:1-10).

This is a mandatory meeting of the whole community, where a member can freely and safely express himself or herself concerning community life. Problems are resolved, misunderstanding cleared up, the discouraged receives encouragement and support. This is a once-a-week meeting; Saturday mornings or at a time set by the director and his leadership team.

Relational Health

Humans are social beings; we are made for relationships. Bad relationships are cause stress, and too much stress is not good for our mental, physical, and spiritual health. The way we behave toward people can add unhealthy stress to their lives. We are therefore called upon to exercise patience, tolerance, and care for each other. Avoid being overly critical and judgmental toward community members.

Conflicts are inevitable, they will happen, and in some cases, conflicts are healthy to a relationship. Conflicts are largely disagreements over needs and perceptions. If there are no conflicts, you will be always saying yes to other people's needs and perceptions to your own hurt. So, there are times you are going to disagree and have to say, no, and that will not be received warmly by others. But it is healthy to express your disagreement without starting a war.

Conflicts becomes unhealthy when it becomes destructive. In destructive conflict, we begin to label people, call them names, wanting to hurt them, so we attack them verbally and physically. This destroys relationship and erect walls of separation. That cannot be allowed in the community because it divides the community into, we versus them. Both sides are enemies to each other, and enemies can no longer share the same place.

A once-a-week group time is suggested for the entire community. It is the time that each community express how he or she is doing. Difficulties, dissatisfactions, and problem are brought into the light and a solution is brought to bear on them. No concern is ignored or brush under the rug; it must be dealt with satisfactorily. Or promise made by director to follow through. It becomes first on the agenda at next group meeting.

Spiritual Health

A person with a health spiritual life is at peace with himself, at peace with God, and at peace with his neighbor. God cannot accept our worship if we hold a grudge against our neighbor. If you bring your gift to the altar and there remember that you brother or sister has a grudge against you or you against them, the Bible says, leave your gift at the altar and go make it right first with your brother or sister, then God will accept your gift (Matt.5:23 study of God's word, worship and fellowship with others, and the breaking of bread. These times set aside are very important and you should not miss them. Without them you could wither on the vine and die spiritually (John 15:1-10). -24; 18:15-20).

Your spiritual health is also nurtured through your quiet prayer life with God, communal prayer,

APPENDIX B

WHEN TO EXIT YOUR HIDING PLACE

Some hiding places might be completely cut off from the outside world, while others are not. Contact with the outside world will all depend on how early you started planning, and the quality of expertise you have on your communication team.

If you do not have a satellite phone and people with cyber and encryption skills or at least ham radio specialist on your team, you will very likely find yourself flying blind. If you have not kept a paper calendar from which you can project yourself into the future, you may also have lost the awareness of dates. But even so, if a record is kept of sunset and sunrises, a person could make his own calendar which would give a good approximation of days, weeks, months, and years. The maximum hiding time is seven years.

The Beginning of Hiding

Most people will have entered hiding, sometimes in the first 3.5 years of the Great Tribulation. Early hiders will have entered the first year after the rapture; somewhat late hiders, the second year, and the late hiders during the third year. Very late hiders are those hiding after the third year; at this time, it is almost too late to hide or pull together a sustainable hiding plan.

However, some people will do it and succeed at it, but it is most risky waiting that late when the odds are just about 99.9% against you. At whatever time you enter hiding, keep track of dates and time. It will prove helpful knowing when to exit hiding.

The Second Avent of Jesus

The second advent is when the Lord Jesus Christ returns to earth with an army of saints and angels to put down the antichrist and his military forces and to establish his reign over the earth (Rev.19:11-21). Chances are—you will see Him descending because it will be visible globally; the Bible says, every eye shall now behold Him (Acts 1:9-11; Rev.1:7). But if your hiding place prevents you seeing this event, you should know that he has arrived from any connection you have with the outside world. It will be a more spectacular event that the rapture. It will be the preoccupation of everyone on planet earth.

Once Jesus has arrived on earth, you are safe from the Beast. But since His arrival will culminate in a World War, you may want to wait a couple of weeks before you abandon your hiding place. It will be safe now to use your communication devices to pick up national and global news, even to contact loved ones. After the war, Jesus will march into Jerusalem to sit on the throne of David to begin His reign over the earth. You may joyfully abandon your hiding place; you will never need it again.

What to Expect Outside

The home you left for hiding some seven years ago, may no longer be there waiting for you. And even, if it is there, it might be occupied by others. If you left families there, they might be dead or still there. If they are dead, it should be a relief; if they are alive, you will have cause to be anxious. You may want to quietly move on without seeing them or them seeing you. Why?

They could only could have survived because they took the *Mark of the Beast.* You will no longer have anything in common with them. This will be painful and hard to accept but that is the very reason you were in hiding all this time. If you are in doubt of this, ask Jesus Himself or any of His ruling representative what their chance are. This could be the only dark moment to the rest of your life.

You see, the millions that have died in the World War are largely military people, ordinary civilians with the Mark of the Beast will still be alive. They will be able to live out the rest of their lives until they die physically. But they are already dead spiritually, they are Satan's property based upon what we now know. Other, than this one bad thing, earth has entered a new joyful era of peace and prosperity, and you are alive to experience it. Not only that, but you also have the guarantee of eternal life. You are one lucky person among billions that have perished or should I say, blessed person.

As for you, you have accepted Jesus as your Savior and Lord, and you resisted the *Mark of the Beast* by going through the difficulty of hiding. You already have the guarantee of eternal life (John 3:16-17). You will go on living out the years of your physical life joyfully serving the Lord. When you die, you will be resurrected and given your new body that dies no more. You should be able to get a good job in the new administration.

OTHER BOOKS BY THIS AUTHOR

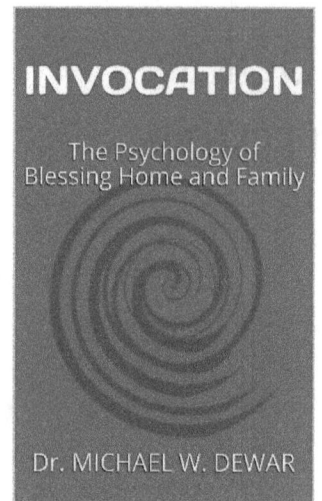

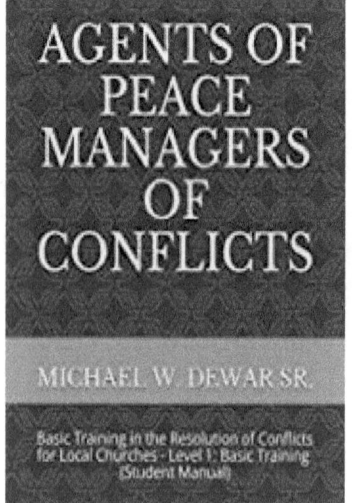
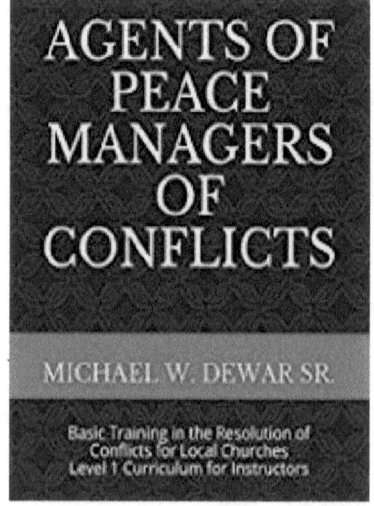

OTHER BOOKS BY THIS AUTHOR

BISCRA-40 is a consumable used for healing, wholeness, and personal flourishing. It is used in a 40-day spiritual exercise set forth in the Eaten Word Book and The Eaten Word Journal. To do the exercise, you need the book, the journal, and the Biscra-40.

THE GREAT TRIBULATION SURVIVAL GUIDE

www.ingramcontent.com/pod-product-compliance
Lightning Source LLC
Chambersburg PA
CBHW071723040426
42446CB00011B/2190